Adventure Book For Teens Fun Things To Do For Teens

Speedy Publishing LLC
40 E. Main St. #1156
Newark, DE 19711

www.speedypublishing.com

Copyright 2014
9781681275505
First Printed January 7, 2015

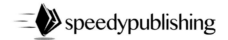

There are
so many fun
things you
can do...

We can play sports for fun. You can grab a partner and challenge each other with tennis, like we always do.

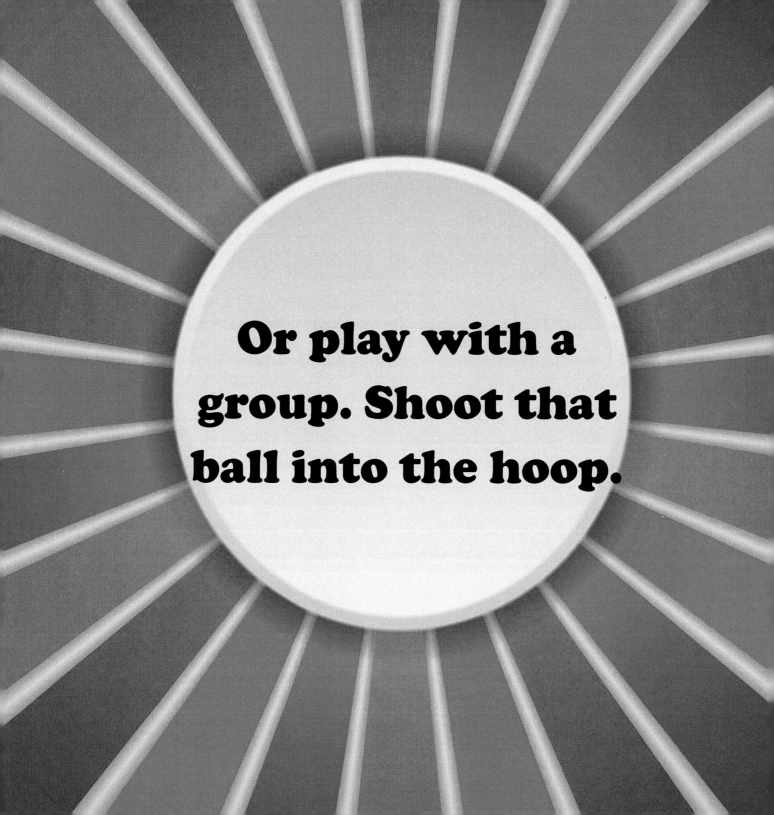

Or play with a group. Shoot that ball into the hoop.

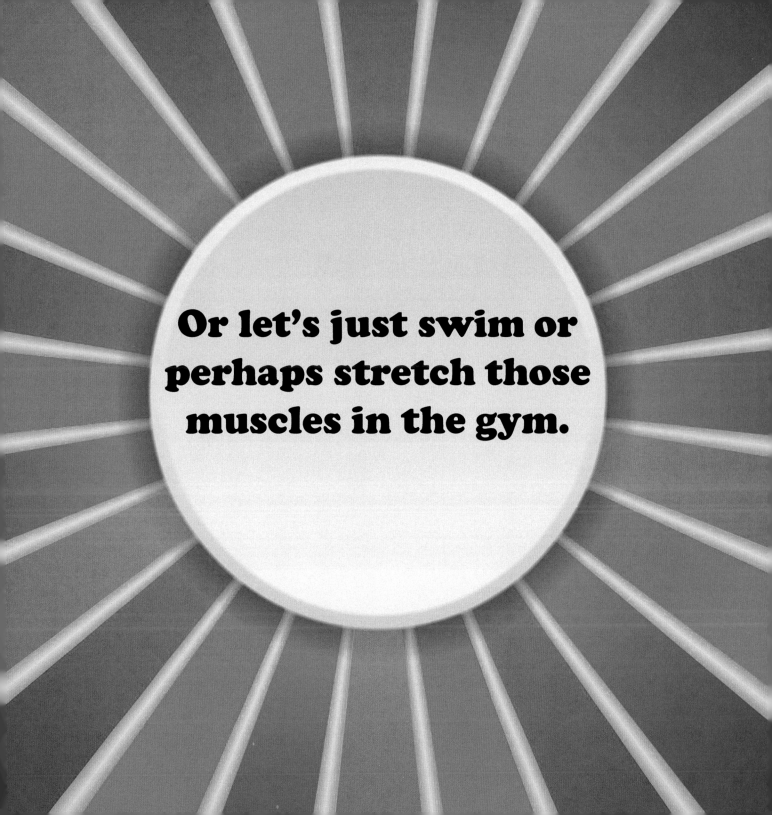

Or let's just swim or perhaps stretch those muscles in the gym.

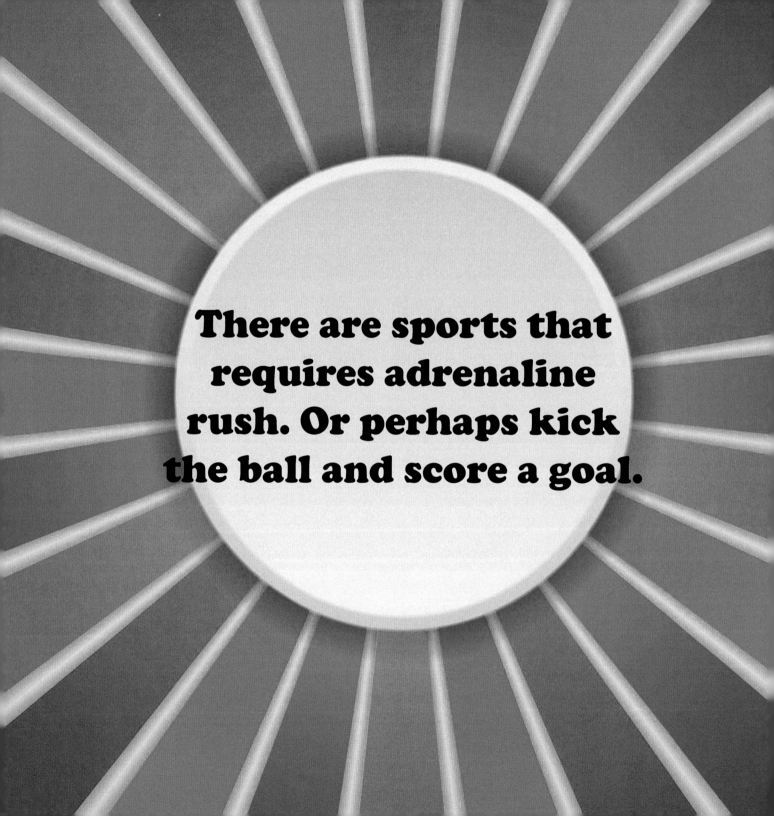

There are sports that requires adrenaline rush. Or perhaps kick the ball and score a goal.

We enjoy fun time with friends. We can grab some paper and pen.

Or share memories

With the a camera,
let's smile and click!

Or sit by the beach, listen to the beat..

Or sing out loud a teenage love song..

We can learn to strum the guitar

Make rythms and melodies, because that's what we are...

Or ballet our way to the ballroom...

to that funky groove...

Stroll, run, or skate...

Most of all, let's have some fun, make special memories, laugh, cry, jump, and run!

Made in the USA
Las Vegas, NV
06 February 2021